CATS ARE CURIOUS

by Paul E. Clark

illustrated by Susan Miller

for Kevin

Published by Willowisp Press
801 94th Avenue North, St. Petersburg, Florida 33702

Copyright © 1995 by Willowisp Press,
a division of PAGES, Inc.

Printed in the United States of America

2 4 6 8 10 9 7 5 3 1

ISBN 0-87406-754-5

Cats are curious...

when you are trying to sleep

and when you are watching
your favorite cartoons

or reading the comics.

Cats are curious...

when you are talking on the phone

and looking in your closet

or answering the door.

Cats are curious...

when you are playing a game

and your mother is calling you to come in

or you are eating dinner.

Cats are curious...

when you are taking a bath

and when you are brushing your teeth

and, of course, when you are
trying to sleep.